Breathe for Me!

Mitchell Chernock

PEGASUS BOOKS

Pegasus Books
8165 Valley Green Drive
Sacramento, CA 95820
www.pegasusbooks.net

First Edition: January 2025
Published in North America by Pegasus Books. For information, please contact Pegasus Books c/o Marcus McGee, 8165 Valley Green Drive, Sacramento, CA 95823.

Library of Congress Cataloguing-In-Publication Data
Mitchell Chernock
Breathe for Me!/ Mitchell Chernock – 1st ed
p. cm.
Library of Congress Control Number: 2020952557
ISBN – 978-1-941859-97-1

1. POETRY / Subjects & Themes / Motivational & Inspirational. 2. FAMILY & RELATIONSHIPS / Marriage & Long-Term Relationships. 3. POE028000 POETRY / Jewish. 4. FAMILY & RELATIONSHIPS / Abuse / General. 5. FAM029000 FAMILY & RELATIONSHIPS / Love & Romance

10 9 8 7 6 5 4 3 2

Comments about *Breathe for Me!* and requests for additional copies, book club rates and author speaking appearances may be addressed to Mitchell Chernock via e-mail to Mitchell@advancedmtg.com
Also available as an eBook from Internet retailers and from Pegasus Books
Printed in the United States of America

To my brother, Paul

Paul sang to me throughout my entire life. When there was a storm in our home, he would sing one of his favorites, "You'll Never Walk Alone" or "MacArthur Park".

I was blessed with "Swing Low, Sweet Chariot" a few days before Paul passed away.

In 1975, Paul called and asked me to leave work early to see him sing opera at The Villa Roma. There was a second floor to the restaurant where they had balconies, and my brother was singing "la donna e mobile" from Rigoletto, when I entered the main floor.

That night changed my life forever, when Paul introduced me to a group at a table who invited him to sing at their home later that evening. In the group, I met an amazing woman named Durell, a woman with magical powers. Durell still has a spell over me.

Thank you, my brother, I love you and miss you.

.

Durell: 1976

Durell: 1976

My first surprise was to be invited to Durell's home for a glass of wine and some music. I was in for thousands of surprises, and what a ride it would be, an E ticket to the adventure park of my life! After the introduction of her 17-year-old daughter, I wanted to ask her age – instead, I made a bold confession.

"I'm 21."

"I'm 38," she laughed. "Come on, you're kidding me, right?"

The easiest thing for a silly young man to do was show her my driver's license. She flashed this incredible devious smile; her eyes told me everything I would need to know for the rest of my life. We took turns being the Flint and the Striker and went well past sparks flying. The result was fire, lots of fire!

Breath of Life

The moment you are blessed by God to conceive a child; He places a beautiful soul in your womb. In the miracle of life, a heart forms, beating with the rhythm of God's Song.

When your baby is born, your child's first earthly blessing is the "breath of life." From that day forward, every breath we take is a gift.

Sometimes, the world gives us so much beauty and so much ugliness at the same time that we lose our ability to breathe.

We ask, *Will you Breathe for Me?*

Gen 2:7

Genesis 2:7 And the LORD God...
breathed into his nostrils the breath of life...

Breathe For Me!

Inhale

Rescue
**I shared my soul.
Together…
we were saved**

Rapha 2
BloodThorn 4
Beautiful Wreckage 6
We Are Lost 7
My Immortal 9
I Discover You 10

Redemption
**I gave my anger to God
the night my father passed away.
I felt his love fill the empty spaces**

One White Rose 13
My Discovery 15
Mirror Image of an Old Soldier 16
PTSD Saint Vitus Dance 20
Men 26
My Shield 28

Loss
**She smiled
Scars crying blood,
eyes wide with terror.
I could feel her deep hatred of men.
Men took her power,
leaving her broken**

My Daughter's Angry Pleasure 31
Green Dress 32
Shards of Anger 34
Bright Red Spot Diary 35
My Daughter 39
Blood Diary 41

From the Heart
**The moment your lips touched
my neck,
my heart was no longer mine.**

Breathe for Me   44
Our First Poem   47
Falling   49
Joyful   50
Gardenias   51
Kiss My Neck Again   53
First Kiss   55
First Kiss Forever Kiss   56
I Kept My Promise   58

Mystery of the Garden
**God planted all the beauty of the world
in his garden where souls grow.**

My Psalm   60
Golden Butterfly   62
Golden Wings, Return to the Garden 63
Nature's Gift   65
Heron   66
Hummingbird   67
Our Beginning   68
Garden of Golden Wings   69
Gift of Butterflies   70

Secrets
She trusts me,
I am the secret keeper.
She knows all her secrets are safe in my care.

My Seasons of Love 72
Jasmine 73
You 74
Champagne Bubbles of Love 75
Renewal 76
Love Melts 77
Our Last Secret Kiss 78
With Child 80

The Light Behind the Dark Cloud
The sun rises beyond the sea.
The world is new again.
The sun is the bright blessing of a new day
exploding in the dusk of the sunset sky

Tears 82
Land Mine 83
Fog 84
Bridge of Ruin 85
A Vision of Black Wolf 86
Dragons 89
Cigarette Blues 91

Abracadabra: Aramaic, avra k'davra
I Will Create What I Speak
My words are a gift from the creator.
I am blessed to share his creations with you.

Moshe in the Desert Garden 98

Exhale

Prosaic Living Words
Acknowledgements

L'chaim
To life
יהוה
YHWH

Preview: *The Sacred White Horse*

Rescue

I shared my soul.
Together…
we were saved

Rapha, The God Who Heals

My faith…
  my physical body,
   my life,
are prisoners in a bed of thorns.
My blood rains red on the soil below.

  My beloved…
You are beneath the thorns,
hidden away in God's Earth.

I have risked my life,
  my battered soul to find you.
Sharp thorns cut,
  exposing my heart.
You are my beloved.

  Blood rushes from my body,
I push deeper through the vines.
  Rapha,
 God the Healer
   heal my beloved.

Buried in the blood wet earth,
I find your heart,
  You are my beloved.
Rapha's hand in my hand,
  I caress your heart.
Another caress,
  another,
Your heart beats…
  You are alive,
   you give me life.

Reaching up to me,
you pull me in.
My soul is alive,
my heart is yours.
You are my gift from
Rapha.

I am healed,
Rapha,
God the Healer,
I am redeemed.
Rapha,
you have healed my beloved.
Rapha…
I am yours

BloodThorn

The moment we met,
the BloodThorn was born
under a white rose,
hiding beneath its petals.
Close to the bloom,
a protector,
ready for your sacrifice.

You gave me a rose
with *one* thorn
on a perfect long bare stem,
a drop of your blood on the thorn.
I wondered if it was… your sacrifice,
a purposeful act to prove your love.
To leave a single bloodstained thorn,
a reminder,
          beauty can be dangerous,
love so treacherous.

This beautiful white rose is bound to the bloodthorn.
the same as we are bound to each other.
We are the same as the long stem rose,
          beautiful,
                    dangerous,
                              forever treacherous.

In the fire of our love,
          we lived in secret.
Every day, waiting to be stuck,
          to bleed.

The fire of our love
made the bloodthorn sharper,
            dangerous beyond our desire.
We are dangerous,
        a single burning kiss
changing our lives forever.
        I am in a joyful dance,
        living in a lifetime waltz.
We are the rose.
        We are the BloodThorn,
            beautiful,
                dangerous,
                    yes,
            forever treacherous.

Beautiful Wreckage

We have battled for an eternity,
        surrendering to an endless struggle
of love and redemption.

My life is blessed in your wreckage,
        remade in your soul,
resurrected… in your love.

You,
        you are a powerful angel,
my secret lover.
        Give your wings to me;
I will surrender my heart to yours.
You can have my mortal power
by giving up… your immortality.

I will share my earthly soul with you;
Share with me your heavenly body.

        Accept my heart and live,
I will be your last breath of immortality.
        I will be the last beat of your Immortal heart.
        Take my breath,
take my breath and breathe.
        Take my heart,
take my loving heart
        to live… a mortal life.

We Are Lost

Our bodies are so close,
I feel your touch.
Your heart beats far from my heart.
Darkness hides our love,
the light from your soul
no longer guides me.

I fear we are lost.

The angry mother in you sees me as a child,
she's taken away your love,
and your sweet caress.
She's closed your eyes to my heart,
          to my love.

I fear we are lost

You sleep in my arms,
you are a ghost,
          I reach for you.

I hear voices,
storytellers in my mind,
telling me your love is dying,
screaming inside me,
Mourn her loss,
her love is dying.

I refuse to believe the voices are right.
You are with me,
I can hear you breathing in the silence.
I feel your breath on my face.
I hear your heart beating,
I inhale your beauty,
your sweetness.
I am renewed in your scent.

We are timeless travelers,
brought together across an infinite universe.
I can't resist
a simple touch in the night.
My hand in your hand.
My heart stops,
I hold my breath.

I fear we are lost.

Lying next to you,
a magical feeling,
exploding my senses.
Each time I inhale your perfume,
your love permeates every part of me.
Your last kiss
lifeless, filled with anger.

I can't resist,
our hands touch.

Have we lost our power,
Power that pulls us together,
Power to fight for each other,
A love we cannot fight against?

With our first kiss,
        deep,
life affirming,
        an awakening of our love,
                buried deep within hearts,
                        waiting to be rediscovered,
                reborn in the memory of
                        our first kiss.
Are we lost?
        Another touch,
                my hand in your hand,
                        fingers clasp,
                                lips touch. **Gen 2:18**

My Immortal

My immortal,
     my beast,
          my love…
               my eternity.
God's beauty sparkles in your emerald eyes.
     Across the universe of time,
we meet again,
a forever kiss sealing
     our eternal life together.
You are my timeless treasure.

We turn to dust,
     we rise.
         You are my immortal.
We turn to dust,
     we rise together,
        we are immortal.
The ages rage against you.
     You are a beautiful force,
        relentless,
           unforgiving.
Love is your spirit,
     your kiss a dagger.
Your power is life and death,
     I am slayed by you.
I am your immortal.
     Together we rise,
        you are my beast.
           Together we rise,
        you are my eternity.
     Together we rise…
        We are… *immortal*

I Discover You

Are you my mysterious sly lover?
Are you a fun prankster?
Are you the laughter in my heart?
I discover a new part of you every day.

Your eyes,
shy and devious.
Your heart,
always on fire.
Your tongue speaks with mystical power.
Your words are secretive and elusive.
I know better.
           What a discovery you are!

Adventure is yours,
dangerous and spontaneous,
you constantly surprise,
your quick wit angers.

I see your loving eyes,
I hear your heart,
beating with desire.
I see you sparkle
across the room,
eyes twinkling
across the universe of my life.
You are heart-stopping,
I discover a new you with every kiss.

I am slayed by you,
I die each night in my sleep.
You bring me out of the darkness,
I am reborn at sunrise.
The scent of your body
breathes life into my flesh.
Every day, I learn to love you.
What will I discover today?

My father's love for me was immense,
I learned from my father's
pain to love deeply.
Somehow
he taught me to love
from my soul,
to have an open heart,
how to do more than hold on,
to keep my forever promises,
to renew my love for you.

I discover you.

We have become new,
we touch,
we embrace,
we kiss.

The heat of your body melts my resolve.
Teach me   to love you.
Teach me   to laugh with you.
Teach me   all ways to touch you.
Teach me   to speak your poetry.
Teach me…
I will be your forever student.

Redemption

**I gave my anger to God
the night my father passed away.
I felt his love fill the empty spaces.**

One White Rose

One white rose remains
in my mother's garden.
Her petals are new,
crisp with morning dew.
No thorns protect
her delicate flower.
This last sweet white rose
is born in the softening of age.

It has begun.
It's time for my brother and sisters
to pray for mother to enter
the garden of God's love.

Days filled with many joys
will forever be remembered.
White rose petals,
bathed in sweet tears of love and loss.
Tender as a single new petal,
our mother waits to see
her lost lover.
He waits in the garden of their youth,
where my mother's sweet petals
were blessed by God.

My mother blooms
in a new eternal life
yet to be.

I know my father is reaching down
from heaven to take your hand
into the boundless love of God's heart.

In the passing moments,
Mother will join my father.
Her last earthly breath
        a sigh of God.
Heaven will open,
        welcoming the beautiful soul
of a new angel.

Walking together in the garden of their youth,
        lovers will repeat
        their wedding vows,
        married by God into eternity.
                One white rose blooms
        in the garden.

My Discovery

Here is where the boy fell asleep.
I forgot the boy was still here,
tucked away safely.
I left him hidden in the stairwell,
where my sisters and I hid
during my father's storm.

My gentleness,
wit and spontaneity,
all the parts of me,
I thought I could not keep.
I left them in the stairwell.

The boy talks to me in a daydream.
I have grown to become the good man,
I... am a good son

Today I rescue the boy
hiding in my past,
living in my heart.
It's the right time for him to awaken.

Today
          I am a lucky man,
                    today…
                              I am the boy!

Mirror Image of an Old Soldier

The boy in my dad's heart
reflects in the mirror,
stroking his gray beard.
He smiles at the shine
remaining in his boyish gray eyes.
He wonders if the man he has become
can ever be like the boy he once was.

Playful,
joyful,
mischievous in so many ways.

Aches and pains have conspired
to take the boy's happy and hopeful memories.
For a time,
he is bound and gagged
until old age pain reprieves.

Inpatient,
the hint of recovery
brings out his curiosity.
Can I sleep,
can I sleep in?
Am I better today,
can I have some fun?

All the boys who knew him
                    saw an old soldier,
                    A Father,
                    A crossing guard,
                    The food sampler,
                    Teacher,
                    Boy scout leader,
                    Fisherman,
To fish with my dad one more time.

The old boys who once knew him
have left for God's great sea.
He prays,
allowing himself to see his sadness.
Seasons flash by in moments.
A summer of fun brings out
a shimmer in his old gray eyes.
Dad had one more summer
at Camp Royaneh with the boys,
raising our flag ceremonies,
        merit badges,
                campfire stories.

Celebrating 84 years of living,
he listens to stories from old soldiers
at the Vet's home.
A thousand old soldiers will die today...
A truth echoed in the hallways,
        1000 old soldiers will die today.

In a moment of clarity,
he knows his time will come soon.
Fall gives way
to winter's foggy dark skies.
In late October,
we went fishing one more time
before he gives into his weak and weary body.

We are at his side,
a final kiss for his boys.
In his final moments,
entering eternal sleep,
he smiles.
He knows the beauty
of the rough road he has traveled is over.

He hears the voices of his boys
whispering their permission to go sing and dance
with the angels.

Mirror Image *Epilogue*

A late December cold day
calls this old man to God's great sea.
Flying proudly in his memory,
I salute the flag honoring his service.
All his boys will miss him,
　　　　none more than me,
the boy of a father whose heart remained forever young.

*PTSD Saint Vitus Dance

New Guinea
256th Coastal Artillery Group

Cannons blasting their discontent
towards our fierce enemy.
Our big guns angry reports
echoing back at our firing team.

The ground shook with every man's body,
feeling the shock of each round fired,
every man finding a place
within themselves to hide
from the horrific onslaught,
climbing into a hole,
praying soon the shelling would be over.

A cratered pit,
their place of fearful refuge.
When our boys came home,
they brought the cratered pit with them,
remaining within their battered hearts
for all their mortal lives.

Malaria married my father
following him into the mud and muck of life.
He sank into darkness with war and fever.

It was lights out at home
for fear of an attack by the Japanese.
He was in my mother's arms,
his hands shaking,
his body trembling with panic,
angry love his only outlet.
I witnessed angry love every day.

My father's cratered pit
was deep and ugly.
He took his first-born son
into the pit with him,
to lie underneath the sludge.
If you look inside the dreadful ooze,
you'll find a man and his boy
who've lost their way.

I have fathered a damaged son,
deformities I can see,
frailties of a father's lineage.

He looks at his sad reflection
in the mirror.

My glass is empty.
I have survived war.
I came home.
I feel loss.
I have attacked my boy
while searching for a way
out of the darkness.
My boy's bruises
will remain deep within him for all his life.
I am not a weak man.
I don't understand my anger.

In a room of lost and damaged men,
we hear the drumbeat.

Shellshock is temporary.
In a man's world
they say iron sharpens iron.
Iron prepares men for battle.

I hit my boy again.

I fell into the pit with my father,
the dark pit,
face-down in the mud and muck.
My life crumbled,
falling with my brother into darkness.

War buddies visit.
I hear their voices,

Be strong,
fight the demons.
Good men
don't beat their sons.
Good men
don't beat their sons.

All I could do,
all I could think,
all I could hear,
"Good men don't beat their sons!"
I screamed into the darkness,
"What the fuck?"

I rolled over in the sludge
to see the wet slippery walls
holding me down.

Father cries out in the pit.

I hear my son call my name.
He is here with me in the pit,
my son holding me in his arms,
begging me to release
the dying man inside me.

Father,
don't let my brother drown.
Don't beat him.
You are broken,
my brother has been broken,
I am broken.
Love me!

Father slips further into the darkness.
I can hear his voice,
I can't see him
buried in the muck of anger and loss.
My brother cries,
I see their shadows.
They are holding each other.

I wanted to be a better man for you,
you've always been my damaged boy!

Darkness comes again,
my loss is so deep.
The walls widened,
I fell further into the muck.
I am the good son,
the undamaged son,
the anointed king,
the unbeaten son.

Father's pain lives inside me,
every memory I have lingers.
I can hear his voice
in the stillness.

I love my boys,
I love my sons.

My father rose
out of the mud and muck to see me
in a sudden moment of awareness.

Together…
take your brother's hand,
you can climb your way out.
I'm here.

My fingers go deeper
into the mud and muck
holding me down.
I stood on the falling debris
crumbling in front of me.
Father is looking down,
the light from his eyes
showing me the way out.

I sank again.
His hands reached out to pull me up.
All my anger slipped away.
We rose up to stand on solid ground.
My father has me,
I have been found,
I have been saved.

Together we pulled my damaged brother
into Mother's shining light
showing us the way home.
My father's cratered pit
has lost its power over us.
Darkness and light,
anger and love,
shadows passing each other
in life's final act.

In his last years,
his last days,
he loves his damaged son.

We rose out of the darkness together.

Holding my father's hand
in his last moments,
he whispers.

My sons,
       my boys,
I am rising out of the cratered pit
Shema Ysrael

A last kiss for a damaged son,
a last kiss for a good son,
the last breath of a loving father.

Men

We keep our pain a secret.
We think no one knows.

They ignore us,
call us toxic.
Our eyes tell a different story,
a portal into our masculine souls.

Our hearts know no boundaries,
our bodies pushed
beyond the physical.
Our souls, our souls are beautiful.

From the beginning we are flesh and blood,
tools used and tossed away,
left bruised and broken.

There is a distance in your gaze,
the ache,
the angst of loss.
We are scorned,
no different than a physical insult.

We live in quiet desperation.
My war,
my battle,
I can't breathe,
I fight for truth,
I struggle for a truce.
Relief cannot be born in my death.
How can I live?

Invictus is my chant.

> *In the fell clutch of circumstance,*
> *I have not winced nor cried aloud.*

      I want to cry out loud,
            I must,
yet I can't.
      Pain is my Hell,
my bondage.
      Pain
      is my dreadful true connection to reality.
Can I be healed?
I am real,
      I feel pain,
           I know loneliness,
I pray to God,
      I pray for strength,
               I… am unafraid!
I… can be healed,
      I… will be healed,
           I am blessed,
               I… am a man!
           You are blessed
              you will be healed,
                  we will all be healed.
We… are men

My Shield

I am a king,
I am a man,
I am mortal,
I... am not a god,
     I am not a god.

My shield... is battered.
My body,
my body has taken its last blow.
My shield has defended its last strike.
     I have given my full measure.

My enemies gather around me,
they stare,
they stand in disbelief.
They have found
     I am simply a man,
nothing more than they are,
flesh blood and bone,
all the same.
We are the same.

I am a king,
I am a man,
I am mortal,
I... am not a god,
     I am not a god.

Kneeling before my enemies,
striking my sword into wet earth,
I pray for a swift and honorable death.

My enemies have seen their own glory
in my will to fight for God.
Holding my last breath of life,
I see the armor of a conquering king.
The sound of his blade
on my blade brings life.
A king's sword,
        pushed into the earth,
steel on steel,
two swords,
one nation
        joined together in final battle.

I am uplifted,
I am revered,
I am free,
I am reborn.

Together,
we are men.
        We   are all kings!

Loss

She smiled.
I could feel her deep hatred of men.
Men took her power,
leaving her broken

My Daughter's Angry Pleasure

Sharp blade,
        cutting,
                release,
                        exploding ecstasy.
                                No more pain.
Healing begins,
        scars remain,
                scars remind,
                        too many memories.
                                Secrets kept.
Empty bottle,
        my secret,
                pain hidden,
                        always angry.
                                Sad memories.

Release,
        one more time,
                desperation,
                        pain.
                                My pain.
Old and new,
        forever part of me,
                empty promises.
                        Empty bottles.
Battle scars
        my battle scars,
                empty bottles
                        One   day   sober.

Green Dress

I heard him slam the car door,
the tempo of his walk.
My stomach churned,
my legs wobbled.
Angry keys fumbled at the lock.

I wore the green dress...
He never liked that dress.
He's home,
there is no time to change,
no place to hide.

For a moment,
the house breathes in
an eerie silence.
Like the pause
nature takes in the storm,
before it shoves a flying tree
up your ass.

I've been called worse names.
The smiling girl inside me
began to cry.
She scorned me.

I told you not to wear the green dress!

One hand grabbed me by the neck,
the other by my hair.
Echoing in silence,
I can feel his breath on my face.

Vodka, I hate vodka!

*Whore! I warned you
not to wear the green dress.*

My knees buckled again,
my power to run
draining out of me
like a dying animal.

Everything blurs,
my head bouncing on the floor,
the green dress covering my face.

Whore! echoed in the silence

Cotton panties cutting my legs,
my body ripped open.

The sound of a beast
roars in triumph.
Sharp pain,
numbing pain,
sweet numbing pain.

Green sparkles of light
penetrating through my green dress,
his body invading my body,
spiking my soul.

A few moments pass,
all of me,
every part of me wiped out,
changed forever.

I hate the green dress,
I hate that green dress.

I hate that bastard!

Shards of Anger

My life has been broken!
    My body invaded!
Beaten and bruised!
    I must run.

Shards covered the floor.
    Shiny,
glistening,
      begging me to run.
No safe passage.

Bare feet,
    running,
        bloodletting,
    Escape!

He can't catch me.

    I am immortal,
I bleed,
    I am flying,
I am free!

    Looking back,
I see him,
    he sees me.
I *see* his evil.

      Fuck you!
I am free
    I   am   free.

Bright Red Spot Diary

So many years ago
    I was 14.
The Smiling Girl lost
charge of my life.

She was raped.
    We were raped
        I was raped.

I tucked her away with all my happiness
        deep in the darkness,
beyond the reach of my nightmares.

    Naked.
Looking in the mirror at my reflection,
my blood drips from 1,000 cuts.
    Unrelenting pain,
my own beautiful pain,
    my gratification of blood loss.

I can see my scar from the first cut,
    a reminder of my strength,
raw courage
    covering the truth of my weakness.
Touching each jagged scar
makes them new again.

The beast raging in me has gone silent.
My blood-stained blade hidden
in my bedside drawer.
In a daydream I hear her voice
    crying in the darkness.
In a moment of rage and revelation
    I pull back the curtains.

Light penetrating my darkness,
    she is exposed.

She has been found.

     She commands me to open my eyes.

Look in the mirror

     Lost in my dream,
she smiles for me.
     I am smiling,
my first in many years.
The Smiling Girl is here.
     She has risen from the darkness,
taking me with her into the light.
She has risen!

Angry voices in my head,
     silenced by her laughter.
Go,
go outside.
     You are no longer invisible.

I promise I won't,
     I promise.
          I promise I won't.

The bright sky has been a heavy blanket.
Voices are louder,
     people talking and laughing.

Hello. Hello? my neighbors yell.

People can see me.
     I can see them,
their homes,
     my neighborhood,
my hidden life.

The Smiling Girl rises inside me.
     My arms waving,

I say "hello."

> *I'm talking,*
> > *I'm smiling.*

My promise echoes in my head.
"I promise I won't,
> I promise.

The fear strangling my joy is gone.
> She tells me our secrets,
whispering to my soul.

> *I feel your pain.*
We feel our pain.

> Sobriety is agony.
The Smiling Girl stirs my soul.

> *I am real.*
You are real.
> *You are mine.*
Pray,
> *pray for us,*
pray now!

> I don't pray.

> *Yes.*
We do pray

> I don't believe,
I can't believe.

We will,
> *we will believe again.*

I am praying,
> I promise I won't use again,

God,
I promise I won't use again
    I need your help
        I am praying

My Daughter

I cried on the eve of creation,
yelling in silent pain,
my body invaded,
left in my own darkness, like garbage.

My tears fell again
when I felt my soul come to life.
I am more than one,
        I can never
        be more than one.

I heard my baby cry
on the eve of shadows.
        She cried for me,
                for my weary soul.
She came to me in a dream,
        lifeless,
a ghost child.

Do you want me,
        will you love me,
                will you take my life?

I cried on the eve of destruction.
My mother called me.

        I love you.
Honey, what's wrong?

I heard my baby cry.

You don't have a baby.

Yes, she lives inside my body;
her blood flows through my heart.
        She knows can't keep her.

In God's light,
darkness holds on to me.
My eyes are open,
I see a vision of my baby,
protected by the hand of God.
She walks with angels.

My friends say it's okay to kill my baby
            (Everyone does it)

This is *my* truth,
I can feel her living in every part of me.
In my dreams, my baby cries,
she screams at my soul.

            Let me live,
                    I am your gift,
a gift from God.

My senses are keen.
Inside my body,
her heart beats
with the music of life.
            A rhythm,
her song,
            her heartbeat,
our song of life,
            my daughter.

Appointment cancelled,
            life affirmed.
My daughter.

Blood Diary (OCD)

Listen to her voice.
          Is she the Smiling Girl,
the lost good girl?
I pray she is not
the bad girl.

Both want me,
          argue over me,
invading my sleepless dreams of
night and day,
bickering over control of
my weak soul.

Your hands are dirty.
          Wash those dirty hands!

I washed the paint off the walls,
          the skin from hands,
the memories from my broken mind.

Cutting,
searing pain cleanses light and darkness,
gathering dust,
an empty bottle hiding in my drawer,
a reminder of my teenage terror.

My body,
          ripped open,
 releasing the bad girl,
          imprisoning the Smiling Girl.

Sleepless nights
wait for a new bottle.

Never again,
   one day at a time.
I don't hate myself,
I want my life back,
   One day at a time.
I don't hate myself,

   I'm taking my fucking life back!

From the Heart

**The moment your lips touched
my neck,
my heart was no longer mine.**

Breathe For Me!

When I first saw you,
I breathed in your beauty
        so deeply,
I could not exhale.

        The scent and power
of your drug leaving me limp.
I can't breathe.

        Breathe for me.

The moment you spoke,
        your words were devastating,
crushing me,
        paralyzing me.
I could not retreat.
        You laughed at my heart.
Did your eyes lie to me?
I can't breathe.

        Breathe for me

Your sword is sharp and swift,
        like your tongue,
casting a spell.
You take away my breath,
        you stop my heart.
My love magic is useless.

In a moment of weakness, we touch.
        I hear you inhale.

Is it my scent?
                    Is my scent a drug?
Am I an intoxication?
 I can't breathe.
            I can't breathe!

            Breathe for me!

My breath is trapped in my chest.
            You are my drug,
your beauty is my weakness,
            you are my intoxication.

You try to escape,
            an accidental cheater.
We touch,
            we touch,
                    a brush of fate,
your hand on mine.
            You catch your breath,
and for a moment you soften.
            I   am released from your spell.
I exhale,
            I am dizzy.

Your defense is love magic,
            a spell you cast
to destroy men's hearts.
I can't breathe.

            Breathe for me.

I am not made from steel,
            as I am a man.

Because I desire your spell cast upon me,
you become weak and vulnerable.
The weaker you are,
the more powerful my love becomes.

I am powerful!
Let me breathe for you!

I see your battered shield,
     I know your battlefield.
          Your smile hides the beast
I have tamed deep within your heart.

     In the waterfall of my love,
your beast is washed away,
     your heart is cleansed,
your heart is cleansed.
     You are mine,
I am yours
I will breathe for you.

     Will you breathe for me?

I will breathe for you.

     Will you...breathe for me?

Our First Poem

When I wrote our first love poem,
we danced,
            we kissed,
you swooned.
Rosé!

You whispered again and again,
your words touching my soul.
Rosé, Rosé!

You kissed my neck,
            wrapped your arms around my body.
I spoke the words
I love you.
You kissed my soul.
Rosé!

Tell it to me again please… please?

Yes.

Through a glass of wine,
to see your face,
gorgeous you are.
Slipping through sweet aroma,
I taste your scent.
After wine, you are a joyful bubble.
To float with you is heaven.

We dance slowly,
    a soft kiss.
    we never let go,
a forever kiss,
    we never let go,
        not for a lifetime.
            Rosé!

Falling

My love is the ancient river,
        flowing into the mist.
Gentle at first,
        then a raging tempest,
roaring over the edge.

        I keep falling,
falling moment by moment,
        falling into the abyss,
praying to be lured by you,
        saved by you.

Your love is different,
                tormented, jagged,
        sharp rocks jutting out
from the falls.
        Thunderous torrents
wash over you.
        The falls reveals shadows,
silhouettes of your body in rainbow mist,
        shadow warriors protecting you.

My life is a continuous
fall into deep water.
        The mist is blinding,
the mist is revealing.
        You are the tempest,
you are the thundering storm,
        a river without end.

Night comes.
For a moment your body is revealed
        in the glow of a yellow moon.
You are beautiful,
        you are my timeless traveler.
You are my most powerful savior.
        Take me into your waterfall.

Joyful
She saw my walls collapse,
my resistance fading.

My heart is stolen.

How she laughed at me!
her body shaking with joy.
She smiles,
          she laughs,
she laughed again.
          Not *at* me.
                    No!
Not at *me*
Not from being snide or cynical.

Oh how she laughed again!
She knew she had me.
          She owned me,
heart,
          mind,
                    body and soul.
I am hers for a lifetime.

Joyfully,
          I am yours
                    for all eternity.

Gardenias

Gardenia petals float
in a crystal bowl
by your bedside,
their scent permeating the night.

A sweet dream unfolds.
       Beautiful flowers,
brave hours,
       love that grows,
moonlit morning silence,
       love's essence.

              You take my hand,
              a dream of long walks
              in the sand.

Our love is as gentle
as angel's wings in flight.

Soft breezes wake my senses.
A sweet caress,
       a forever promise,
       everyday beginnings,
       love without endings,
       gardenias perfumed the night.

Sleep comes again,
remnants of my dream dance,
such a beautiful romance!

Your body glistens in soft moonlight.

A sweet caress
a forever promise,
everyday beginnings,
love without endings.

The scent of love,
gardenias perfumed the night.
Gardenias,
gardenias perfumed the night!

Kiss My Neck Again

Our first touch,
         our first dance,
                  our first deep breath!
         So many years ago,
I smelled your scent,
         tasted your perfume.
You kissed my neck.

Our love is forged in fire.
You strike my soul on the anvil of eternity.

I was afraid.
You were bold,
Courageous.
         You were the first.
         I love you.

You melted my resolve,
         frightened me,
blinded me
         One touch,
                  one kiss,
                           I am yours.
         You let me see you
with all your magic.

         Kiss me,
                  kiss my neck again.

The room spins aimlessly without you.
         Everything stops the moment
I see you.

My heart stops,
I cannot turn away from your fire.
Everyone stares,
no one dares to break the flow of our energy

Our wedding song plays,
                 we are young again
        on fire more than ever.
You kiss my neck
       I remember our first dance,
              you kissed my neck.

You cast a spell,
       we are forever in love.
Play our song again,
     kiss my neck
          once more.
               I am yours,
     kiss my neck again…

First Kiss
          An invitation.
Next dance—
          slow dance.
Hands touch,
          bodies embrace.

Our eyes close,
          our noses touch.
Instantly my heart is yours.
          Inhaling,
          lost in your embrace,
          breathing in
          a dizzying scent of jasmine.
Moist lips,
          secret smile,
                    your eyes open for a moment.
You whisper,

          Yes…

          A shiver,
                    a chill.
Soft skin shimmers.

          Perfect!

Sparkles in the night…
          our lips caress.
                    Wow.
          One perfect kiss!
Inhaling,
          breathing in
                    the dizzying scent of love.

First Kiss,
Forever Kiss

My heart beats in my throat.
    Holding my hand,
you whisper,

    I want to kiss you.

I couldn't breathe.
Our first kiss is branded on my heart.
    I can magically taste
your lips,
    intoxicating.
An anniversary of new love.

    Tonight,
a new first kiss,
the kiss of our engagement.

Kneeling,
I show the sexy smile you love,
in my hand a golden box.

I remember you softly saying,

Yes,
holding out your hand,
waiting for me to slip a new treasure
onto your finger.

We are transported back in time
to our first dance,
          your skin smells like jasmine.

Our hands touch,
I feel your breath on my neck,
          You whisper

          Yes.

Your lips on my skin,
          your lips on my lips,
my heart…
          in my throat.

I Kept My Promise:

I fell asleep on your grave,
        woke up in your loving arms,
kissing your soul.
I woke up in a daydream
I'm dancing with your shadow
to our song.

We are an opera,
        an endless musical love story,
one continuous fire in the opening act,
        joyously resisting Act II,
tirelessly resisting the end of Act III.

It's all a waking dream.
        I kept my promise
You are dancing on clouds,
        singing to the stars
illuminated by moonbeams.

I felt you again last night,
        inhaled your scent,
touched your skin,
        kissed your face.
You are my timeless treasure.

I kept my promise, my love,
        I kept my promise.
I am not broken,
        I am not sad,
I am not lost,
        I am,
Am I?

Mystery of the Garden

**God planted all the beauty of the world
in his garden where souls grow.**

My Psalm

א [Aleph]

My time in heaven ended
            when God prepared
me for my earthly journey.

He created the land world,
the sea world,
the mountains and sky world.
God the made the plant and animal world
and called it Earth.

God took the essence of Earth,
creating man and woman.
            Earth blossomed into a multitude
of his precious children.

Humankind will have their seasons.
            Together we will
            fulfill God's destiny
            on the land and mountains,
            in the oceans and sky.

ב [Beth]

I am the Hummingbird,
soaring in the eye of a hurricane.
            My wings beat
to the rhythm of the storm.
I alone control the wind,
            sent by the Creator.
I know nature's force,
fanning the flames of life.
He extinguishes those
flames with one breath.

He is mine throughout the seasons,
He
          is wind!

I came from the sky,
          God gave me wings,
I walked the way of the sun,
          God gave me his everlasting light,
I walked the way of the stars,
          God showed me the heavens,
I walked the way of the moon,
          God gave me the tides of the seas,
I walked the way of the seasons,

God blessed me ... with Earth.

I am the Hummingbird,
          I am the great eagle,
                    I am the lamb,
                    I am ram,
                              I am the lion,
I am the minnow,
                    I am the whale
          I am the flower,
I ... am the great redwood
          God blessed me with earth.

Golden Butterfly
For my boy, Jeremy

In my dream,
there is a beautiful garden.
The garden is tended by a goddess.
The goddess holds
within her caress,
a Golden Butterfly.

His wings now open,
the Golden Butterfly
has remained with the goddess
for many years.

My dream continues,
        I am in the garden.
My heart pounds with joy,
        my mind is a whirlwind of anticipation.

The goddess releases
the Golden Butterfly.
As he flies to my waiting heart,
        his gilded wings
        become arms and hands.

I welcome my son to manhood.

When I wake in the morning,
        I find the golden wings of
a boy in the palms of my hands.

Golden Wings, Return to the Garden:
The loss of my father

On the path of dreams
that really do come true,
there are golden wings
waiting for you.

A boy who learns to fly
becomes a man,
a father who touches the sky.

There are golden wings
waiting for you.

As a father, he sits in the garden
with his young son.
He wonders of himself as a boy,
of his own childhood,
filled with joy.

A boy who learns to fly
becomes a man,
a father who touches the sky.

In the calm wind
an angel came to say,
Tell your boy
heaven touched your wings.

As you passed by,
       God whispered to your heart.

Golden wings wait for you
in the garden,
in the garden of the goddess
where you became a man,
       golden wings wait for you.

A boy who learns to fly
becomes a man,
a father who touches the sky.
       My father has returned
       to the garden of golden wings.

This poem is dedicated to my father (12/29/1999) and those who lost
their lives on the Space Shuttle Columbia (02/01/2003)

Nature's Gift

Mother,
I am your daughter,
          I am your flower.
Mother whispers to me
          of her beginning,
of her joy,
her love for God's precious earth.

I am the flower
          created by God.

Mother is the soil
where I grow.
Mother is the rain,
nourishing my earthly body.
Mother is the sun,
warming my heart.
Mother is the talking wind
telling stories of my beginning.

Mother feeds me,
          I bloom,
                    I am beautiful.
We are beautiful.

My wilting petals tell a story
of my ancestral beginning.
I am
the story of a mother's first flower.
          She is
          Earth's gift
          created by God.

Heron

Gliding across blue sky,
      soaring in God's beauty.
The land world is yours,
      calm water is your solitude.

You are blue and glorious white.
      You float softly to the shore,
a gentle assassin, drifting in grace

A ballerina,
your beautiful body,
          a silhouette at dusk.
Your long neck,
      a delicate question mark,
       reflecting in water's mirror.

In life's gift,
      you danced the dance of love
with your mate,
      giving birth to a new generation.

You are a huntress on a secret mission,
      your attack is swift and effortless.
You are timeless,
      you walk on water,
         you float on the wind.
You danced the dance of love.
      You...
           are Heron

Hummingbird

Born in God's storm,
soaring through the eye of a hurricane.

Forged in the heavens to become a warrior,
my wings beat faster than my heart,
flying towards the sun.

Courage is the magic of my being,
my joy,
        is nectar.

Watch me dance on raindrops,
drink from flowers swaying in the breeze,
chase bees away from my blessings,
bathe in small pools of joy.

My feathers are made from
starlight and moonlight,
cast into the river of rainbows.

Recollections of my life's journeys
stay with me for all time.
Memories of a flower's nectar,
memories of a raindrop,
memories of love,
stay with me.

Our Beginning

In the days ahead
created by God,
the sun and moon
pass each other in the orange dawn,
again in the purple evening dusk.

Poetry is the fire in your soul.
Psalms of the Kings,
Words of the Prophets
will guide your heart.

We are two souls
meeting again.
For a moment the world stops,
everything beautiful in its place.

We have found each other
in the vast sea of souls.
Searching for love,
we married in Gods ritual
for all eternity.

We will share the night
beneath a hidden moon.
All our days
in the glow of a rising sun.

Garden of Golden Wings

God's garden surrounds me,
          His beauty is everywhere.
This is the place
my mother brought me to life.
Mother gave me golden wings,
igniting the spirit in my soul.
          A path leads far beyond the horizon,
too far for me to see the Tree of Life.

Holding my mother's vision in my dreams,
the garden is filled with joyful beings.
Golden butterflies,
dancing from beauty to beauty.
I hear laughter,
playful boys searching for manhood,
boys waiting for their fathers
to welcome them into the company of men.

Mothers teaching their boys to be men,
giving their boys the gift of an eternal heart.
A heart waiting to be broken
is redeemed with a mother's love.

Only when my boy
sheds his damaged wings,
will he enter a new world,
dancing in God's most
          beloved transformation.

Boys becoming men…

Gift of Butterflies

When I was a young boy,
there was a secret meadow
in the mountains above our camp,
a place to be at peace
with my creator.

In the springtime,
when the buffalo came
to the high grass,
I would go there,
treetops surrounding this sacred place,
forming a circle in the shape
of a chief's war bonnet.

In the meadow,
there is an ancient spring.
This is where my heart is reborn
each time I return.
Small sweet flowers grow
in the rainbow mist.
When the sun drops below the horizon,
thousands of butterflies come to rest
upon the sweet petals.
Closing my eyes
I would lie still in the mist and wait.
Soon I would be covered
in a blanket of butterflies.

A beautiful gift from the Creator!

Secrets

**She trusts me,
I am the secret keeper.
She knows all her secrets are safe in my care.**

My Seasons of Love

Solstice ends
with the birth of Equinox.
Colors of the Fall drift in the wind
       on a gray and white day.
Beauty is replaced
       by a cold gray fog,
a mixture of gray and white,
       persisting on my somber moods.

Leaves swirl about
       until caught in silent rain.
Hidden buds wait in bare trees
for their explosion of color in the Spring.

Only bright light remains
       from the warming rays of sun,
shimmering on icy puddles,
       refusing to melt.

New footsteps of winter
have found a path
in the few remaining days of fall.
There are memories of love
in the leaves,
floating on the wind,
washed clean by the rain,
silenced by fog,
memories,
       memories of our seasons,
          memories I have kept.

Jasmine

Tonight
you smell like jasmine.
          Your touch
ignites my senses.

You are a gentle small flower,
your scent
          sweet with mystery.

Tonight
you are a wild vine
          encircling my loving heart,
                    entwined in my soul,
tied to our vows of forever love.

Tonight
          you smell like jasmine,
your scent
          sweet with mystery.

You

Our angry love trickles
through the hourglass.
Memories falling into our past.
A dream ends,
      another begins.
Do you long for hot summer days,
sandy beaches,
      my touch,
           my kiss,
my unconquerable soul?

You are a raging ocean,
then a calm sea.
Your eyes glisten against the waves,
wet hair clinging to your face,
      covering your beauty.

Has December left you cold?
Will my fire be enough
to warm your soul?
Thoughts of you fill my head.
Will you listen to my poems of love?
Can I touch your heart?
      Will I be your forever lover?

A dream ends,
      another begins,
dreamer…
      Are you a dreamer?
I dreamt of you last night.

Champagne Bubbles of Love

A toast to my love,
one sip, you giggle.
The taste is magnificent,
lips wet with champagne.

Taking a deep breath,
more bubbles of joy,
the bottom of the glass.
Swallowing my resolve,
I toast my love,
one more taste,
        no forced smile,
bottles half-gone.

Heat bathes my body,
There is no time to waste.
I feel your hands on my skin,
a touch of silk.
Kisses taste of champagne
from tender lips.

A chilled bottle
against my heated skin
sets my heart on fire.
It's time for more.

The bottle empties,
my body drifts.
Floating in your arms,
our souls collide.

Both spent,
conscious of lingering pleasure.
Champagne bubbles dance on your skin.
I will drink to your love, forever.
        You are an addiction,
                every kiss a first taste.

There will never be a last!

Renewal

You tuck my handkerchief
into my breast pocket,
flaring the folds to perfection,
laughing at me with your mischievous smile.

Standing before me,
          no white dress this time,
Soft, pink,
          above the knee.
You tease,
          bare from hem to neck underneath.

Torrid thoughts walking the aisle,
we are in a playful game,
filled with secrets,
kept silent by forever promises.

Remember our old vows:

Ask for grace,
smile your surrender.

I smile *my* surrender.
New vows,
new secrets.
I will keep your secrets,
          I promise.
I promise I will keep your secrets.
          I am the secret keeper.

Love Melts

Powdery snow swirls at our feet.
We run,
          we slip,
we make it to the door.

Drifts of snowflake cotton
float across the floor,
evaporating in the heat of our passion.

Fingertips so cold they ache.
The fire in my heart warms your body.
          Toes curl in a blanket.
A roaring fire blazes in the darkness.

Heat floods our bodies,
our lips are cold.
We touch.
          We kiss,
we melt,
          we touch,

                    we kiss,

                         we melt!

Our Last Secret Kiss

Holding your note,
        I smiled,
wondering exactly what you had in mind.

I played the movie
of a rendezvous in my head.

Meeting you at our special nightclub
where we met,
filling me with wild memories of that night
You are a clever creature,
        wearing the skirt,
red cashmere sweater,
 leather jacket
        and red high heeled pumps.

You were dressed exactly as I met you on our first date.
It was an ambitious evening
      ending with one long kiss.
I imagined you had more
than a kiss in your plan,
knowing tomorrow we would be married.

Listening to myself talking to you,
I was quickly saying
why it could be so much fun
breaking the rules.
I could see you enjoyed torturing me.

Our favorite bartender
gives you a thumbs-up.

You were as magical as ever.
The moment I heard Percy Sledge,
I knew you were toying with me,
singing the words,
When a Man Loves a Woman.

Our chosen wedding song is playing.
We are on the dance floor,
        your hands on my waist.
Just before the song is over,
        you pull me tight to your body.

My heart is in my throat,
        you whisper to me,
Our last kiss before we are married.

A kiss to last for an eternity,
        your lips pushing on my lips,
your hand squeezing me from behind,
our last secret kiss.

Our song ends with your smile,
escaping from me,
running to the door with a joyous laugh.
        Our rendezvous…
        for one last kiss.

My heart is in my throat.

With Child

Your radiant smile,
        your playful secretive laugh,
you hold me tight,
        ready to unveil a mystery.
Holding my hand on your face,
        you hold my other hand on your tummy.
Happy tears cascade,
        I need no words.
You open your robe to me,
        exposing your naked body.
As I kneel before you,
        your eyes shine with more tears.

    Our daughter will arrive in the fall.

I kiss your tummy,
        my daughter's first kiss,
Our first embrace,
our first kiss acknowledging God's gift.

I am more in love than I can imagine.
        In my soul,
                I hear you whisper.
We… are blessed.

The Light Behind the Dark Cloud

The sun rises beyond the seas.
The world is new again.
The sun is the bright blessing
of a new day
exploding in the dusk of the sunset sky.

Tears

Winter road the wind
until she lay heavy upon us.
She was bitter cold,
                angry.

Sister Sun had gone to sleep.
Winter snuck in
with her white blanket.

Skies opened,
        snow fell,
                tears fall,
                        silence.

Our tears are a reminder of the walk
        on the trail of death.
Our memories are carried
in the talking wind.
Stories of our oral traditions,
passed from generation to generation.

        We will never stop
telling our stories.
        We will never forget.

Tribute to Princess Diana

Cool mist floats down through the trees,
        white blinding fog,
waiting for sunrise.

Evil lives in the ground
beneath the mist,
        patiently waiting
for a moment in eternity.

Piercing through heaven's gate,
        rays of sun point the way
on the path of no return.

Children playing,
        laughing and running,
filled with life.
        Wet earth
        heaves in the new dawn,
                bursting under
barefoot children,

        their souls
                scattered red
against
        the white mist.

Land Mine

Fog

She's a blinding temptress,
her grey
covers me in cold mist,
her heavy white
blankets me.

Hiding shadows of her past,
she wears a damp coat
of salt and sea.

Fog hovers,
hiding the distant horizon.
She hides the raging seas.
Fog shrouds the seashores
with their rocks of death.

She fears most
            the sun-driven wind.

When fog's veil recedes,
towering cliffs rise into the sky,
rejoicing in the white mist of
crashing waves
against the shoreline rocks.

Sheer walls
            repelling the sea's assault,
She provides no safe refuge.
            She… is fog

Bridge of Ruin

Take a drive down the long eerie road,
a daydream turning into a nightmare,
        a dark dream in the thick fog
where the Beast carries a heavy load.
Cold white fog hovers
on the never-ending edge.
It is the blinding dreary
shrouding the old Martin Bridge.
        His creaking beams
            singing like sirens on the rocky shore.
Mystery flows under chilly waters
waiting patiently beneath
the Beast who calmly waits for more.

Reflecting at himself in the icy mirror,
moaning and gloating at his image,
        always waiting,
                always foreboding.
Soon icy shoals soon will melt
under warm cleansing rays,
revealing his secrets, carried in the talking wind,
        secrets from foggy blinding days.

He is revealed for a moment,
his ugliness steel-gray
against the white mist.

Shadows of his deceit lay dead
beneath calm chilly waters.
He gloats and moans in the wind
as the Beast reflects back at himself,
            gloating,
                moaning,
                    waiting.

A Vision of the Black Wolf

Before there was humankind
on Mother Earth,
there was a great battle.
The four-legged
fighting the trembling Earth,
the Wind spirit,
the Fire spirit and Rain spirit.

The four-legged called on their creator
praying for him to bring forth
shadow creatures of the night
to save Mother Earth.

Black Wolf rises
to command his army of Shadow warriors.
Brother Wind roars
his dominance over all beings.
The wolves howled
with the power of the Creator
commanding the Wind Spirit,
forcing Brother Wind
to turn on his Sister Rain,
extinguishing Brother Fire's flames.
Together Fire Spirit and Rain Spirit
returned into the sky world.

The Creator commanded
the Earth Spirit to bring peace
to the four-legged.
The animal world is victorious,
the storm has lost.

A blanket of snow protects
Mother Earth while she heals.

Black Wolf,
leader of the Wolf Clan,
kneels in the snow,
his black fur speckled white,
he bleeds.
His blood runs red,
staining Mother Earth.
He howls at the orange dusk.
Black Wolf mourns the loss
of his mother and father,
sisters and brothers.

He knows Earth will bloom again.
The ancient voices of the talking wind
have foretold a prophecy to him.

*There will be two-legged
sent to Earth by God.*

He has seen the coming of a
woman in a dream.
She will bring peace to the sky
land and sea.

Black Wolf opens his eyes,
the prophecy is true
Mother is here.
she kneels in the snow
she bleeds.

She paints her face red with her blood.
His blood flows.
She whispers to him,
I am *Earth Mother.*
He lays against her body,
She lays over him,
healing him.

She bleeds for Black Wolf,
her blood mingling with his blood.
She is born again…
He is reborn within her,
     she is Earth Mother.
She is …
     Mother of all living beings…
          of all living things.

Dragons

Stars call to me…
        I can hear their testament.

The millennia has treated you well,
Dragon,
we wait for you.

        The stars are brighter tonight,
        they call to me.

        Dragon,
we joyfully wait for you.

It's been centuries since I blew fire.
        It takes a lot out of me.
I am past the age of desire,
        I am mystical,
                I am Dragon.

My life is power,
        my power is fire,
I am Dragon,
            powerful over all.

I have magic,
        I command the sky,
I burn for joy,
        I blow fire at enemies
standing in my way.

I am the mystery,
born in the fire of God's will.
My spark diminishes day by day,
from starlight to sunlight.

Soon I will return home to the stars,
called back to the place of my birth.
I am past the age of desire,
		I am mystical.
I am Dragon.

		I am a new star on the horizon,
I have been reborn in God's sky.
		I am... Dragon

Cigarette Blues

Each puff is different.
The taste is old and somehow familiar.
When I wait too long,
my craving washes away my sanity.

My mouth
shaped in a pucker,
blowing smoke,
exhaling relief from my lungs.
My ever-wide cheeks expand,
puffing
          inhaling
dispensing
smoke in a straight line.
So cool!

Another drag,
blowing out a perfect oval,
floating smoke rings into the room,
in your face
          in your eyes.
A smile and a look of disgust
comes over you.
The red glare expands more,
flaring with an angry burn,
like a villain in old movie
          in a dark room.

Thick white smoke hovers around me,
follows me wherever I go.

I puff with an audible wheeze,
my cigarette igniting further.
I'm cool
flashing my victory sign,
holding a cig

between my two fingers
like I'm important.

My fingers haven't yellowed
like my old friend's fingers.
I hold my cigarettes with class;
they hold their cigs
like gangsters
within their hands,
hiding a smokey red spark.
Smoke seeps between their fingers,
dancing in the air,
fingernail nicotine stains forever!

Sometimes my cig hangs from my lips.
I lean over,
my eyes watering,
smoke rising
covering my face.
Tears fall
extinguishing the fire of my habit.
What an amazing feat!

Wooden matches scratch the striker,
flame flares,
the smell of sulfur in the air.

The mirror doesn't lie.
Holding my next cigarette,
I caught sight of the fire in my eyes.
An unexpected cough,
flame extinguished.
Is this a sign?
an omen?

A cig unlit
hanging from my mouth,
my cheeks suck in
the dry taste of tobacco.

Hanging from my lips unlit,
I fight the urge to give in.
      Unlit—
is it time for me to quit?

In the mirror
I see the reflection
of an old man in a young man's body.
Not cool!

Unlit,
I pray it remains unlit.
Disgusting,
I love it just the same.
I can do this!
Do I really hate myself?
Can I do this?

Abra Cadabra: I Will Create as I Speak

**My words are a gift from the creator
I am blessed to share his creations with you.**

Moshe in the Desert Garden

Who am I?
I Am…
           like Moses in search
of the Promised Land
beckoning the Jewish people.
I wander on the paths of prophets
in search of the Great Sea.

A sea filled with knowledge
and glory of the ages.
A calm sea with the future
of God's unwritten pages.

The promise of wisdom and glory
glistens on the shores of humanity
shimmering in the sands of time
washed away
by the raging oceans of eternity.

Knowing I foolishly seek
wisdom in the glistening sand,
I desperately search to find my soul
in the great sea raging in my mind.

In the desert
the sun and moon
are as husband and wife
greeting each other in the morning
again in the orange dusk.

Poetry of the prophets speak to my soul.
My words dance in the heat
of the desert sun
coming to life in human confusion.
My life is more than an illusion,
where I am the sand
on the shore of his Great Sea.
I am not the salt of the Great Sea.
The salt dwells in my soul.

The ocean retreats in waves
leaving the cool sands
of time for me to walk upon.
The waters have ceased
to rise above my head,
the retreating torrent
revealing the ancient paths
of prophets.

The waves have softened
no longer washing away
my footprints in the sand.

On the shore
God's book lies open,
its pages crying out.
The quest for knowledge
and wisdom lives and dies
in the hearts
of every woman and every man.
Each has a Great Sea
raging within their soul.

The innocence of my youth
is a distant memory…
I know I cannot rest in the boughs
of the Tree of Knowledge.
I will scale every branch
risking my life
on the ever-new fragile growth
rising above me.

I will continue to climb upward
until I reach the Greatest Sea of all
to discover the salt
that (who) dwells there
for all eternity.

If it is His will
in all He has created
I shall fall.
Then it will be that I rise again
above the land of milk and honey,
rise above the Promised Land,
rise above the land
Moses journeyed to find.

I will enter the Heaven above
all God's earthly creations.
I shall enter His sacred garden
with the soul of one who found wisdom.
For I have scaled….
              the tallest
tree in the garden.

Gen 2:9

L'chaim
To life

יהוה
YHWH

Prosaic Living Words

My dad, George, was a man all about the neighborhood. He made sure every boy on our street who wanted to go camping, fishing, to a sporting event, and enter Cub Scouts or Boy Scouts was able to do so.

When I was 16, I remember being on an elevator with my father when a family came in with a disabled boy. I don't know what happened, but my father, being a Shriner, made sure they took their son to Shriner's Hospital to receive care. I discovered from my father's friends this wasn't the first time he had helped someone he did not know.

He was not the most devout Jewish congregant. My brother, Paul, and I had our Bar Mitzvahs, and our sisters participated in all the holiday traditions. Dad and Mom made sure we went to Sunday school and had a Jewish upbringing. We learned about our traditions and how important we are as people on God's Earth. Shortly after my Bar Mitzvah, I became my mother and father's crazy kid. God or bad, I rarely was found out or disciplined.

Every day at dinner, and oftentimes just out of nowhere, my father would say the Shema. I came to understand something very important: whenever he was feeling out of control or things weren't going right, he would whisper this prayer. When things were going well, he would say it out loud, with joy!

The Shema is my daily anthem to my soul: *Hear, O Israel! The Lord is our God, the Lord is one! Blessed be the name of his glorious kingdom forever and ever. You shall love the Lord your God with all your heart and with your soul with all your might.* ~ Deuteronomy 6:4-5

Shema Yisrael, Adonai Eloheinu Adonai Echad: Baruch shem kevod malchuto l'olam va'ed.

Life Reflection

I grew up a San Francisco native in the 1960s & 70s during the Summer of Love and the end of the Vietnam War. My father, George, was a World War II army veteran in the South Pacific.

He taught me how to be in front of people and to have fun while making new friends. He also told me the importance of having female friends. Later in my life, this lesson proved to be invaluable My mother, Thelma, was a nurse administrator in a convalescent hospital. Even though I was rarely in trouble, she always seemed to be wherever I needed her, and she was thrilled when I made the decision to enter a medical school for respiratory medicine at age 17.

I lived in the storm of my father's Post Traumatic Stress Disorder (PTSD), where my father saw me as the good son, and my brother, Paul, the bad son. Paul had multiple birth defects and was overweight, making him the perfect target for my father. My two sisters were simple bystanders, living with their own dark secrets.

In 1991, my dad decided to tell me he had ruined my brother's life and had to figure out a way to fix their broken relationship. They had a good relationship for the last eight years of my father's life.

The Spring of 1976 marked the beginning of a lifelong journey with my wife, Durell. The most beautiful joy we shared was raising our grandson, Jeremy. My daughter was a meth addict, unable to take care of him, so we raised him as our son. We have been blessed with both of our daughters celebrating many years of sobriety.

Acknowledgements

To my mother and father,
I truly experienced their love for each other for 50 years. Thank you for allowing me to be my own man.

To my brother Paul,
A big thank you for punching me in the face and reminding me you are my brother. I can hear your voice singing every day.

To all the boys who beat me up,
You gave me my own personal Fight Club. I learned how to fight, and you found out I did.

To my 5ᵗʰ grade teacher, Mr. Herron,
You took me from getting an F in science to becoming a Scout Master and helped me become an Eagle Scout.

My wonderful rabbi, Morris,
You graciously made sure I could have my wedding ceremony in the temple on a Saturday evening. You were a true Mensch.

To coach Reed,
You called me a week after my summer vacation started heading into my senior year. "If you want to run track," you said, "I'll see you Monday morning at 7. I had the best sports year of my life.

To my lifelong friends, Dale and Leona,
You helped mold and change me into the man I am today. On the night I met Durell, you were with her, and I know for a fact that you made sure she came after me.

To Rikki and Camara,
Man's best friends. You loved me until you couldn't.

To my boy Eli,
who watches over us every single day.

To Terry Hughes,
my artful friend who produced multiple versions of my book cover. Each time I made a change, the book looked exactly like we envisioned it would.

To John Klysinski, photographer,
You are the man with the eye. You knew exactly how to guide me to create the best image of me for the back cover of *Breathe for Me*.

To every person in my life,
who have allowed me to read stories and poetry to you, even when you weren't interested.

My publisher, Marcus, said to me, "I think we have a book here." We read poetry to each other for 11 months, and we know we had divine guidance.

L'chaim
To life

יהוה
YHWH

Special Preview of Upcoming Work

The Sacred White Horse
told by Ohanzee

Grandfather asked me
to believe in the White Horse.

She will guide your destiny.

I am Ohanzee,
a warrior shaman medicine man.

Everything was white and gray,
a thick blinding blanket on the meadow.
A vision came to me,
I could see through the fog
holding on to Mother Earth.
I was the first to hear them snorting,
talking to each other,
running, playing.
Ghosts floating in the gray
                              white mist.

Horses came to our clan
when my grandfather was a young boy.
Grandfather told me stories
about our times *before* horses,
about his dreams walking with the White Horse.

He taught me these beautiful creatures
are a gift from Wakan
to grow our clan
to follow the great herds
of buffalo across our endless land.

At the end of each story,
Grandfather would smile
and lower his voice to a whisper.

She will come to you, Ohanzee.
You are Shadow,
the one who walks with Wakan Tanka.
Believe in her.
The White Horse will come to you.
She will give you power
to become an honored respected
Medicine Man.
She will give herself to you.

Wind cut the clouds above,
allowing sun's rays to chase away
the blanket of fog.
I could see and sense her medicine
as she walked through the trees.

She led the herd into the high grass.
Covered in foggy mist,
the White Horse,
        powerful,
                beautiful,
standing next to her mate.

Lightning flashed across the sky,
thunder drums echoing,
horses running,
more thunder
coming from crashing hooves.

Grandfather's vison shines on my heart.
Young Warriors are yelling,
"Ponies, ponies!
I want the gray one.
I'll chase him!

Another boy claimed the brown one.

We were ready to chase ponies
and run with the ponies.
They laughed at me
when I claimed the White Horse.

"There is no White Horse, Ohanzee!"
My friends yelled as they ran into the meadow,
the herd scattering in every direction.

In the trees,
I could see her standing with Black.
She was whiter than snow
with a black mane.
He was blacker than the darkest night
with a white mane.

I ran across the meadow
as she came to greet me.
Fog,
		blanketing her,
					protecting her.
I did not understand.

She shook her massive head,
her black mane moving like water.

She talked to me,
her warm breath on my face
as she pushed me back,
her front legs kneeling before me.

Taking hold of her black mane,
I threw my leg over her back.
She stood,
turned and walked into the forest.
Black followed,
I looked to see my friends
still chasing ponies.

I am humbled by my Creator,
Wakan Tanka has given me a gift.
I can hear my heart speaking.

It's time to accept your destiny, Ohanzee.

White Horse and me
are part of each other,
together a blessing from Mother Earth.

We went further into the forest
until we were hidden in tall dark growth,
giants reaching to touch the sky.
Sunlight flashes through the trees,
an eagle soars above,
a hummingbird dances in the wind
coming to rest on my hand.

I knew we were in the presence
of Wakan Tanka.
I asked the Great Spirit
to show me my path.

The wind is speaking to me,

Ohanzee,
You have been chosen

I have been chosen?
I have been chosen.

Mitchell Chernock

Moshe Shalom, son of Joseph,